THE BIGGEST BEST LIGHT

Daniel Darling & Bri Stensrud

Art by Hsulynn Pang

HARVEST HOUSE PUBLISHERS
EUGENE, OREGON

Scripture quotations marked GNT are taken from the Good News Translation in Today's English Version–Second Edition. Copyright © 1992 by American Bible Society. Used by Permission.

Verses marked NIV are taken from the Holy Bible, New International Version®, NIV®. Copyright © 1973, 1978, 1984, 2011 by Biblica, Inc.® Used by permission of Zondervan. All rights reserved worldwide. www.zondervan.com. The "NIV" and "New International Version" are trademarks registered in the United States Patent and Trademark Office by Biblica, Inc.®

Cover design and hand-lettering by Kristi Smith / Juicebox Designs
Interior design by Left Coast Design

For bulk, special sales, or ministry purchases, please call 1 (800) 547-8979.
Email: Customerservice@hhpbooks.com

ᴍ This logo is a federally registered trademark of the Hawkins Children's LLC. Harvest House Publishers, Inc., is the exclusive licensee of this trademark.

The Biggest, Best Light

Text copyright © 2022 by Daniel Darling and Briana Stensrud
Artwork copyright © 2022 by Hsulynn Pang
Published by Harvest House Publishers
Eugene, Oregon 97408
www.harvesthousepublishers.com

ISBN 978-0-7369-8237-5 (hardcover)

Library of Congress Control Number: 2020948553

Printed in China

22 23 24 25 26 27 28 29 30 / LP / 10 9 8 7 6 5 4 3 2 1

In the beginning, God spoke into
the darkness and created a world
full of brilliant light.

God continued to speak, creating flowers
and trees, whales and birds.

He created everything to
live and flourish in His light.

Finally God created something more beautiful
than anything else He had made—people!

God breathed life into this new creation.
He made a man named Adam and a woman named
Eve, creating them uniquely in His own likeness.

They were designed to flourish in God's
light and carry it inside their hearts. This made
them light-bearers—people who could shine
God's light throughout the world.

God made every person in His likeness and said His creation was "very good."

God created everyone to live in love
and peace in His perfect light.

But one day, the light-bearers started making
their own light, a light different from God's light.
They started to think, "My light is better than
God's light. My light makes me better, brighter,
and more important than other people."

They forgot that God didn't create some people
better, brighter, and more important than others.
He made them all equally loved and important.

When people tried to make their own light—
without God—it started creating shadows,
separating them from other people.

As more and more people filled the earth,
these sinful shadows grew.

God never created the world to have shadows
like these, and this made Him very sad.

People discovered that these shadows separated them from others they thought were different from them, unlikable, and less important than themselves.

Hiding people in shadows didn't just make people *feel* more powerful; it made them more powerful in some ways.

Shadows like these create darkness in our hearts, allowing sinful things to grow. Things like selfishness and hate.

This kind of darkness blinds us from seeing God's likeness in other people.

Some people create sinful shadows that
hide people because of their skin color...

or because of their culture...

or because of their
place in the world...

or because of
their abilities.

All of these people, God created in His likeness.

All of these people, God loves.

All of these people were meant to flourish in God's light, living together in love and peace.

But sinful shadows hide
people and keep them apart,
making people fear each other
and forget each other.

The good news is, God remembers all His people.

He never forgets anyone.

In fact, God loves
people so much that
He sent His Son, Jesus,
to turn on the light in our
hearts and break through
all the shadows.

Jesus can overcome the darkness
in our hearts and minds.

Jesus can take away every shadow.

Every person on earth can choose
which light they want to shine.

They can shine their own light, separate
from God, which creates sinful shadows. Or...

they can let Jesus's light shine through them.

If we choose to live as God's light-bearers, we can shine His light into the shadows and see people as God sees them—beautifully and wonderfully made, in His likeness.

The Bible tells us,
"The people who walked in
darkness have seen a great light.
They lived in a land of shadows,
but now light is shining on them"
(Isaiah 9:2 GNT).

With Jesus, we can shine that light!

You can shine His light into shadows
that create fear, by seeing people's beauty
even if they look different from you.

You can shine His light into shadows that create shame, by noticing people who have been ignored.

You can shine His light into shadows that create loneliness, by learning from others and showing compassion.

You can shine His light into shadows that create anger, by loving people even if they believe different things than you do.

Can you think of any people who might feel
hidden because of a shadow someone made?
Is there someone who needs to be seen and loved
better in your family or community? Ask Jesus
to help you be a light-bearer, because seeing
people as God sees them changes everything.

"The light shines in the darkness, and
the darkness has not overcome it."
John 1:5 NIV

"The darkness is passing away, and the real
light is already shining. If we say that we are in
the light, yet hate others, we are in the darkness
to this very hour. If we love others, we live
in the light, and so there is nothing in us
that will cause someone else to sin."
1 John 2:8-10 GNT

"God is light, and there is no darkness
at all in him...if we live in the light—just as
he is in the light—then we have fellowship
with one another, and the blood of Jesus,
his Son, purifies us from every sin."
1 John 1:5-7 GNT

Daniel Darling is the director of the Land Center for Cultural Engagement and the bestselling author of several books, including *The Characters of Christmas*, *The Dignity Revolution*, and *A Way with Words*. Dan is a columnist for *World* magazine and a contributor to *USA Today*. His work has been featured in *Christianity Today*, The Gospel Coalition, CNN, Fox, *Time*, *National Review*, and the *Washington Post*.

Bri Stensrud is a pro-life advocate, writer, and speaker. Her passion is to create resources and content that equip Christians to engage more consistently and tangibly in holistic human diginity issues. She is the director of Women of Welcome, an advocady group for immigrants and refugees, and holds a masters of biblical and theological studies from Dallas Theological seminary.

Hsulynn Pang is a freelance illustrator who specializes in artwork inspired by nature. Hsulynn lives in Kuala Lumpur, Malaysia, with her husband, Sam, and her daughter, Harper.